PIANO · VOCAL · GUITAR

2ND EDITION

JUMP, JIVE, WAIL ... NG

ISBN 978-0-634-00023-2

HAL·LEONARD®
CORPORATION

7777 W. BLUEMOUND RD. P.O. BOX 13819 MILWAUKEE, WI 53213

Visit Hal Leonard Online at
www.halleonard.com

JUMP, JIVE, WAIL & SWING

AC-CENT-TCHU-ATE THE POSITIVE

from the Motion Picture HERE COME THE WAVES

Lyric by JOHNNY MERCER
Music by HAROLD ARLEN

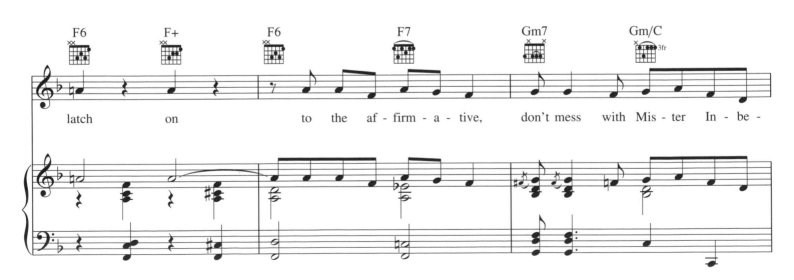

ACROSS THE ALLEY
FROM THE ALAMO

Words and Music by
JOE GREENE

ALRIGHT, OKAY, YOU WIN

Words and Music by SID WYCHE
and MAYME WATTS

Lyrics:
Well, al - right, o - kay, you win, you win, I'm in love with you. Well, al - right,

DADDY

Words and Music by
BOB TROUP

AMOR
(Amor, Amor, Amor)

Music by GABRIEL RUIZ
Spanish Words by RICARDO LÓPEZ MÉNDEZ
English Words by NORMAN NEWELL

BEAT ME DADDY, EIGHT TO THE BAR

Words and Music by DON RAYE,
HUGHIE PRINCE and ELEANOR SHEEHY

BOO-HOO

Lyric and Music by EDWARD HEYMAN,
CARMEN LOMBARDO and JOHN JACOB LOEB

Oh! You mean-ie mi-nie mo, when you let me go, you left me in the mid-dle of next week._____

Once my heart was light and gay, now it's sad and blue, and there is noth-ing left for me to do.

When you said you'd let me go did I hol-ler "No."

I was hap-py yes-ter-day, now I'm so for-lorn.

BOOGIE WOOGIE BUGLE BOY
from BUCK PRIVATES

Words and Music by DON RAYE
and HUGHIE PRINCE

Medium Boogie Woogie

He was a fa - mous trum - pet man from out Chi -
ca - go way, ____ he had a "boo - gie" style that no one
else could play. ____ He was the top man of his craft,

real - ly brought him down be - cause he could - n't jam. ___ The cap - tain
wakes them up the same way in the ear - ly bright. ___ They clap their

seemed to un - der - stand, ___ be - cause the next day the "cap" ___ went out and
hands and stamp their feet ___ be - cause they know how he plays ___ when some - one

draft - ed a band. ___ And now the com - p'ny jumps } when he plays re - veil - le, he's the
gives him a beat. ___ He real - ly breaks it up }

boo - gie woo - gie bu - gle boy of Com - pa - ny B. ___ A toot! A toot! A

toot did - dle ah - da toot. He blows it eight to the bar, ___ in "boo- gie" rhy - thm. He

can't blow a note un - less a bass and gui - tar ___ is play - in' with 'im. _____

He makes the com - p'ny jump when he plays re - veil - le, he's the

boo - gie woo - gie bu - gle boy of Com - pa - ny B. ___ He Com - pa - ny B. ___

CALDONIA
(What Makes Your Big Head So Hard?)

Words and Music by
FLEECIE MOORE

Medium Boogie-Woogie

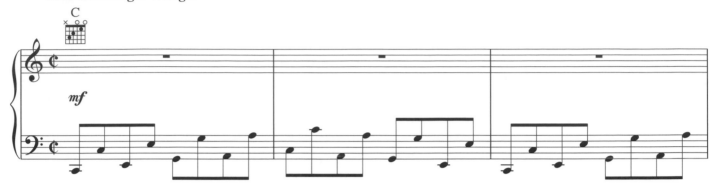

do - nia!   Cal - do - nia!   What makes your big head so   hard?

CASA LOMA STOMP

By H. EUGENE GIFFORD

CHRISTOPHER COLUMBUS

Lyric by ANDY RAZAF
Music by LEON BERRY

Mis - ter Chris - to - pher Co - lum - bus,

Sailed the sea with - out a com -
He used rhy - thm as a com -

- pass;
- pass;

When his
Mu - sic

CIRIBIRIBIN

Based on the original melody by A. PESTALOZZA
English version by HARRY JAMES,
JACK LAWRENCE, PATTI ANDREWS,
MAXENE ANDREWS and LAVERNE ANDREWS

Moderate Swing

Ci - ri - bi - ri - bin, he waits for her each night be-

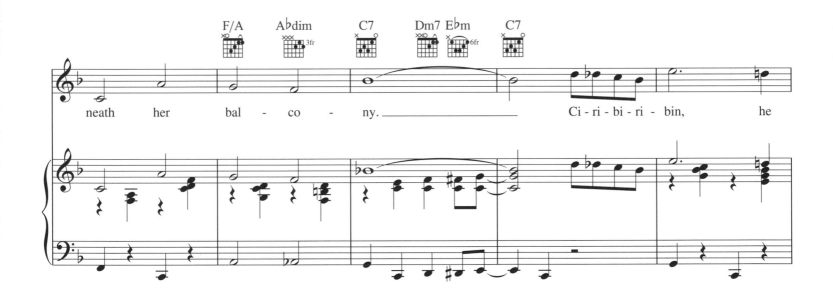

neath her bal - co - ny. _____ Ci - ri - bi - ri - bin, he

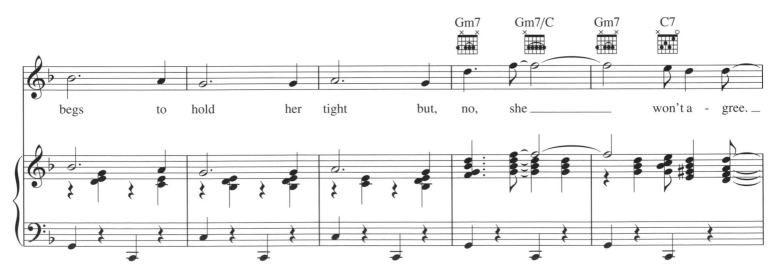

begs to hold her tight but, no, she _____ won't a - gree. _____

DO NOTHIN' TILL YOU HEAR FROM ME

Words and Music by DUKE ELLINGTON
and BOB RUSSELL

Lyrics:
Do noth-in' till you hear from me. Pay no at-ten-tion to what's said. Why peo-ple tear the seam of an-y-one's dream is o-ver my head. Do noth-in' till you hear from

DROP ME OFF IN HARLEM

Words by NICK KENNY
Music by DUKE ELLINGTON

DON'T GET AROUND MUCH ANYMORE

Words and Music by DUKE ELLINGTON
and BOB RUSSELL

Medium Swing

Lyrics: When I'm not play-ing sol-i-taire, __ I take a book down from the shelf, and what with pro-grams on the air, __ I keep pret-ty much __ to my -

FIVE GUYS NAMED MOE

Words and Music by LARRY WYNN
and JERRY BRESLER

FOUR BROTHERS

By JIMMY GIUFFRE

FLAT FOOT FLOOGEE

Words and Music by SLIM GAILLARD,
SLAM STEWART and BUD GREEN

FLYING HOME

Music by BENNY GOODMAN
and LIONEL HAMPTON
Lyric by SID ROBIN

HEY! BA-BA-RE-BOP

Words and Music by LIONEL HAMPTON
and CURLEY HAMMER

I'M BEGINNING TO SEE THE LIGHT

Words and Music by DON GEORGE, JOHNNY HODGES,
DUKE ELLINGTON and HARRY JAMES

never went in for af-ter-glow ___ or can-dle-light on the

mis-tle - toe, ___ but now when you turn the lamp down low, ___ I'm be -

gin - ning to see the light. ___ Used to ram - ble

through the park, ___ shad - ow - box - ing in the dark. ___

Then you came and caused a spark ___ that's a four - a - larm fire ___ now. ___

___ I nev - er made love by lan - tern shine, ___ I

nev - er saw rain - bows in my wine, ___ but now that your lips are

burn - ing mine, ___ I'm be - gin - ning to see the light. ___ I ___

8vb

IF YOU CAN'T SING IT
(You'll Have to Swing It)
from the Paramount Picture RHYTHM ON THE RANGE

Words and Music by
SAM COSLOW

Lyrics:
The con-cert was o-ver in Car-ne-gie Hall, the Mae-stro took bow af-ter bow. He said: "My dear friends I have giv-en my all, I'm

I'VE HEARD THAT SONG BEFORE

from the Motion Picture YOUTH ON PARADE

Lyric by SAMMY CAHN
Music by JULE STYNE

IN THE MOOD

By JOE GARLAND

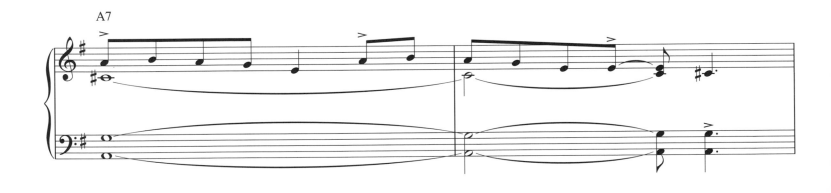

IS YOU IS, OR IS YOU AIN'T

(Ma' Baby)

from FOLLOW THE BOYS

Words and Music by BILLY AUSTIN
and LOUIS JORDAN

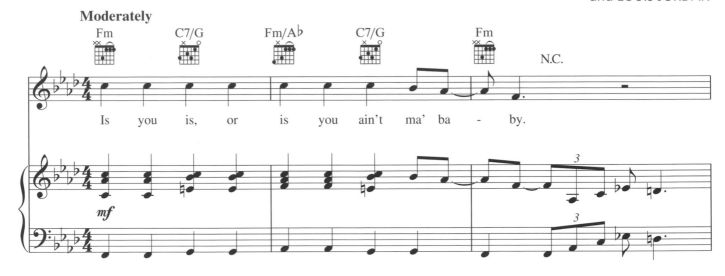

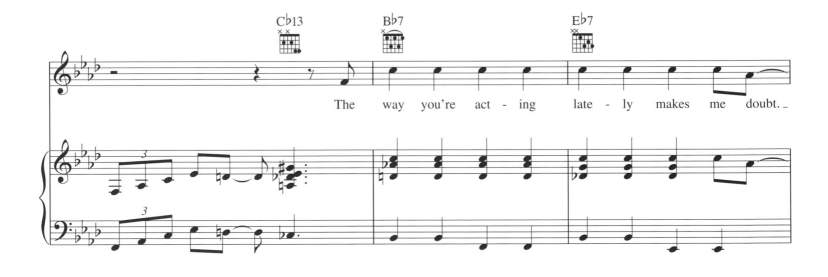

THE JOINT IS JUMPIN'
from AIN'T MISBEHAVIN'

Words by ANDY RAZAF and J.C. JOHNSON
Music by THOMAS "FATS" WALLER

IT DON'T MEAN A THING
(If It Ain't Got That Swing)

Words and Music by DUKE ELLINGTON
and IRVING MILLS

JAVA JIVE

Words and Music by MILTON DRAKE
and BEN OAKLAND

JUMP, JIVE AN' WAIL

Words and Music by
LOUIS PRIMA

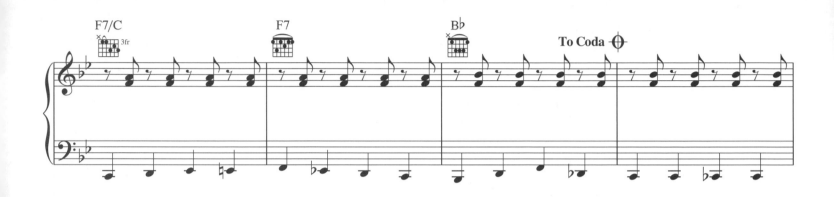

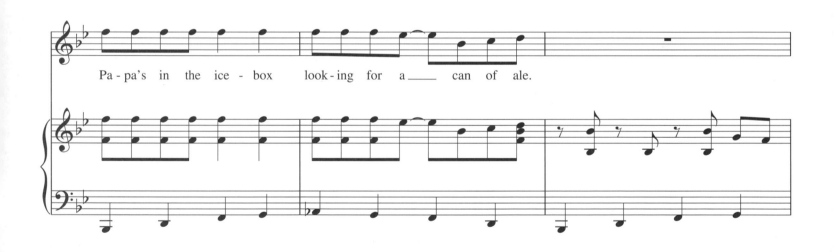

Pa - pa's in the ice - box look - ing for a ____ can of ale.

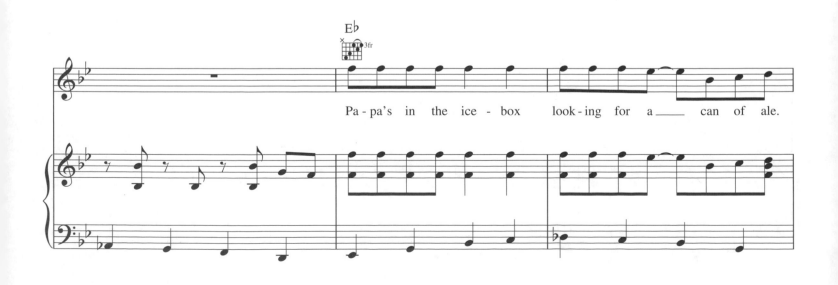

Pa - pa's in the ice - box look - ing for a ____ can of ale.

KING PORTER STOMP

Lyric by SID ROBIN and SONNY BURKE
Music by FERD "JELLY ROLL" MORTON

If you want to get your jol-lies, grab __ your coat and fol-low me. _____ It's bet-ter than a show with dol-lies. Oh, broth-er, just you

LAZY RIVER

from THE BEST YEARS OF OUR LIVES

Words and Music by HOAGY CARMICHAEL
and SIDNEY ARODIN

Lyrics:

I like la-zy weath-er, I like la-zy days;

can't be blamed for hav-ing la-zy ways. Some old la-zy riv-er

sleeps be-side my door, whis-p'ring to the sun-lit shore.

MAIRZY DOATS

Words and Music by MILTON DRAKE,
AL HOFFMAN and JERRY LIVINGSTON

I know a dit-ty nut-ty as a fruit-cake,

goof-y as a goon and sil-ly as a loon. Some call it pret-ty,

MARIE

Words and Music by
IRVING BERLIN

Moderate Swing tempo

There's a

gleam in your eyes, Ma - rie, _____ and the

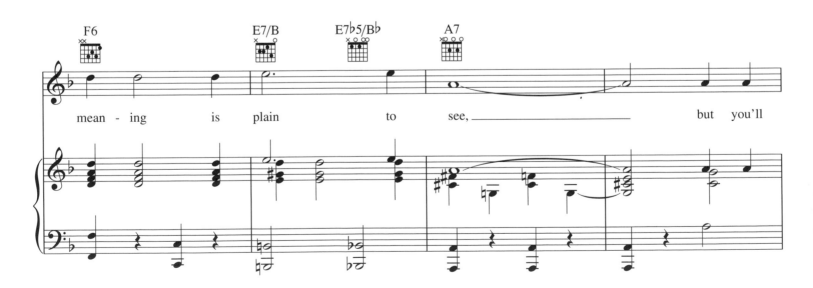

mean - ing is plain to see, _____ but you'll

OPUS ONE

Words and Music by
SY OLIVER

SATIN DOLL

Words by JOHNNY MERCER and BILLY STRAYHORN
Music by DUKE ELLINGTON

RAG MOP

Words and Music by JOHNNIE LEE WILLS
and DEACON ANDERSON

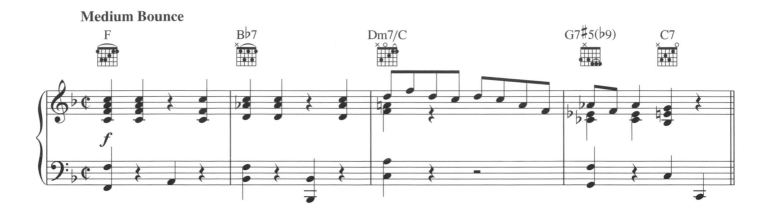

M, I say M - O, M - O - P, M - O -
R, I say R - A, R - A - G, R - A -
A, I say A - B, A - B - C, A - B -
M, I say M - O, M - O - P, M - O -
R, I say R - A, R - A - G, R - A -

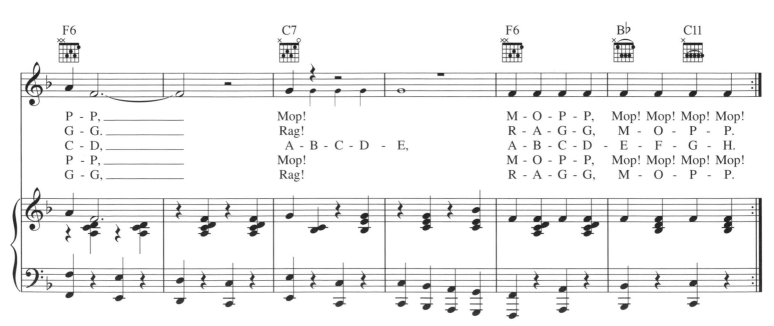

P - P, _____ Mop! M - O - P - P, Mop! Mop! Mop! Mop!
G - G. _____ Rag! R - A - G - G, M - O - P - P.
C - D, _____ A - B - C - D - E, A - B - C - D - E - F - G - H.
P - P, _____ Mop! M - O - P - P, Mop! Mop! Mop! Mop!
G - G, _____ Rag! R - A - G - G, M - O - P - P.

Chorus - *After 2nd and 5th Verses*

ROUTE 66

By BOBBY TROUP

SATURDAY NIGHT FISH FRY

Words and Music by ELLIS WALSH
and LOUIS JORDAN

Solid beat tempo

Now if you've ev-er been down to New Or-leans_ then you can
bud-dy and me was on the main stem,_____

un-der-stand_ just what I mean. Now all thru the week it's
fool-in' 'round_ just me and him._ We de-cid-ed we could use a lit-tle

rock- in'. You nev - er see such scuf- flin' and

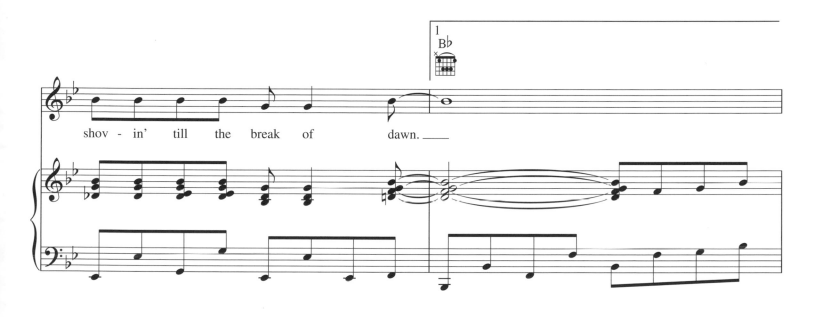

shov - in' till the break of dawn. ____

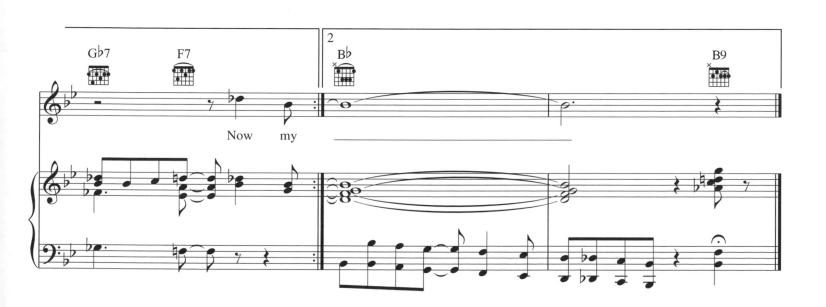

Now my ____

SHOO FLY PIE AND APPLE PAN DOWDY

Lyric by SAMMY GALLOP
Music by GUY WOOD

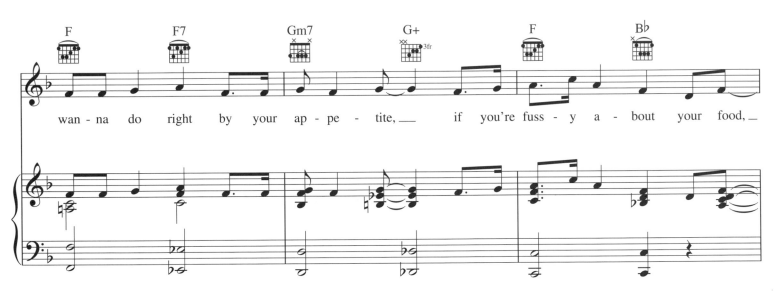

STEPPIN' OUT WITH MY BABY

from the Motion Picture Irving Berlin's EASTER PARADE

Words and Music by
IRVING BERLIN

STOMPIN' AT THE SAVOY

Words by ANDY RAZAF
Music by BENNY GOODMAN,
EDGAR SAMPSON and CHICK WEBB

'TAIN'T WHAT YOU DO
(It's the Way That Cha Do It)

Words and Music by SY OLIVER
and JAMES YOUNG

TAKE THE "A" TRAIN

Words and Music by
BILLY STRAYHORN

THAT OLD BLACK MAGIC

from the Paramount Picture STAR SPANGLED RHYTHM

Words by JOHNNY MERCER
Music by HAROLD ARLEN

WOODCHOPPER'S BALL

By JOE BISHOP
and WOODY HERMAN

Bright Boogie tempo

ZOOT SUIT RIOT

Words and Music by
STEVE PERRY

Recorded a half step lower.

Classic Collections Of Your Favorite Songs

arranged for piano, voice, and guitar

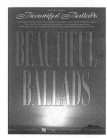

Beautiful Ballads

A massive collection of 87 songs, including: April in Paris • Autumn in New York • Call Me Irresponsible • Cry Me a River • I Wish You Love • I'll Be Seeing You • If • Imagine • Isn't It Romantic? • It's Impossible (Somos Novios) • Mona Lisa • Moon River • People • The Way We Were • A Whole New World (Aladdin's Theme) • and more.
00311679 ....$17.95

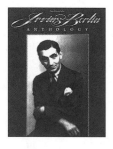

Irving Berlin Anthology

A comprehensive collection of 61 timeless songs with a bio, song background notes, and photos. Songs include: Always • Blue Skies • Cheek to Cheek • God Bless America • Marie • Puttin' on the Ritz • Steppin' Out with My Baby • There's No Business Like Show Business • White Christmas • (I Wonder Why?) You're Just in Love • and more.
00312493 ....$22.95

The Big Book of Standards

86 classics essential to any music library, including: April in Paris • Autumn in New York • Blue Skies

The Great American Songbook – The Singers

Crooners, wailers, shouters, balladeers: some of our greatest pop vocalists have poured their hearts and souls into the musical gems of the Great American Songbook. This folio features 100 of these classics by Louis Armstrong, Tony Bennett, Rosemary Clooney, Nat "King" Cole, Bing Crosby, Doris Day, Ella Fitzgerald, Judy Garland, Dean Martin, Frank Sinatra, Barbra Streisand, Mel Tormé, and others.
00311433 ....$24.95

I'll Be Seeing You! – 2nd Edition

A salute to the music and memories of WWII, including a year-by-year chronology of events on the homefront, dozens of photos, and 50 radio favorites of the GIs and their families back home, including: Boogie Woogie Bugle Boy • Don't Sit Under the Apple Tree (With Anyone Else But Me) • I Don't Want to Walk Without You • I'll Be Seeing You • Moonlight in Vermont • There's a Star-Spangled Banner Waving Somewhere • You'd Be So Nice to Come Home To • and more.
00311698 ....$19.95

Lounge Music –

Ladies of Song

This terrific collection includes over 70 songs associated with some of the greatest female vocalists ever recorded. Songs include: Cabaret • Downtown • The First Time Ever I Saw Your Face • God Bless' the Child • If I Were a Bell • My Funny Valentine • One for My Baby (And One More for the Road) • The Way We Were • and many more.
00311948 ....$19.99

The Best of Rodgers & Hammerstein

A capsule of 26 classics from this legendary duo. Songs include: Climb Ev'ry Mountain • Edelweiss • Getting to Know You • I'm Gonna Wash That Man Right Outta My Hair • My Favorite Things • Oklahoma • The Surrey with the Fringe on Top • You'll Never Walk Alone • and more.
00308210 ....$16.95

The Best Songs Ever – 7th Edition

Over 70 must-own classics, including: All I Ask of You • Body and Soul • Crazy • Fly Me to the Moon • Here's That Rainy Day • Imagine • Love Me Tender •